VIA COMBUSTA

Printed in the United States of America

ISBN 978-1-941561-28-7

Book + Cover Design *by* Angelo Maneage

www.newamericanpress.com
newamericanpress

VIA COMBUSTA

SARA FETHEROLF

Milwaukee, Wisconsin
newamericanpress

CONTENTS

△

QE

ALCHEMY LESSON

Here are the woods where grow ivy & snakeroot.
Here are the woods where grows your mother's house

after she lost it to the bank: the sunlight-hole
where the chimney once stood, the swarm
of butterflies & lighter-fluid fumes.
The door you stood at, waiting for her to unlock it
& let you back in. Tell how you remember it:

it was Mischief Night. You had the head of a dead
man weighting your canvas pack. Here are the woods
you walked through, hearing him on your back,
singing in a forgotten language.
It was Mischief Night. The ivy practiced

catching fire. Tell how to transform like that:
by root & fume & whatever tongues you carry.

TALK BACK

Be thistle & briar & tigerlily
growing roadside. Be skunk or fox or coy-
wolf, sly enough for cities. God says don't

look in the mirror to watch yourself cry,
don't pretend you're a sailor to kiss

other girls, don't dawdle in the bathtub,
playing Melusine. Don't say trauma when

you can tell ghost stories, & if you must
remember, do it silently. Fuck that—

be mouth, still talking when you're told not to.
Be sly. Be poisonous & sharp. Behave

as if the night sky needed to hear secrets
to form the moon each month, & then unform it.
And you, inked & bound with secrets—what luck!

WE MOVED AROUND A LOT

I forget which town it was
            I was in shorts slapping
            deer flies on the walk
to A&P, when a semi first bullfrogged
its horn at my ass
            & for a beat

I thought I'd made the signal
            my brother did once
            on a highway somewhere,
leaning out the backseat window
miming at every truck we passed
            to tug the cord

that unplugs the airhorn's valve
            & they all answered, all
            opened a blast at us
until Dad realized the prank,
pulled over & took him
            into the tall grass roadside.

Then it was quiet.
            Us women waited
            in the buzz of locusts
& cars ripping past.
One slowed to ask
            if we needed help.

I don't even remember where we were going.
It was America. We moved around a lot.

And even then I was lookout, even then
            I kept a weather radio
            by my bed, tracked cyclones
big as semis bearing down on us,
but only learned later
            I was in a more specific danger

—pubescent pigtailed about to be
        bodied—all along
        I'd been working a secret signal
of storm-worry & new-grown ass:
drag that thing down,
        boy, come on, make it sound.

In the second town it rained live minnows. They flickered in the school parking lot, storm fresh. Mom worried the high-tension wires would give us cancer. The library was mildewy, with lead paint. I read all the Nancy Drews. I didn't know it was cicadas making the mystery buzz above; I suspected the high-tension wires. I read *Night of the Twisters*—his house hauled into the air, away, while the boy waits in the basement.

They say it sounds like a train in the distance. They say the drains make a sucking sound. The air turns green.

.

In the second town I wasn't afraid of anything yet. If there was a ghost, I wanted to see it—peered up the chimney, where it swooped & panicked like a trapped bird. Drip stains, names carved at the back: *it looks like a tombstone in there*, I told my brother. Overhead, the mantle clock quivered & shot off its nail.

Mom lay on her made bed—the cornfield was too big; she had a headache to look at it. She said we made the haunting up, but hid the clock in the basement.

.

That year the siren went off 6 times, but the town was always safe. Once, the radio said waterspouts had crossed the Mississippi, but they never came. Fishing in a flooded campsite, Dad caught a monster pike. Its meat tasted saltless, rivery, hard to explain.

IN THE BEFORE

My mother & I played Thumbelina
at the supermarket. I fit in her purse
just about. I dangled my legs from the cart.
        Only & not oldest daughter, I
        was a thimbleful of saffron then, not
the unbrushed girl she scolded later,

coming into the kitchen to find
I didn't know how to sweep properly.
The broom, unwieldly tall man I danced with,
        hoping if I entranced that skinny djinn,
        & made him eat breadcrumbs from my palm,
the house would never go to wrack.

Atticked, I pined to meet a swallow
who loved me for the crumb I was,
& flew me over the river valley rooftops
        (we were in the East by then),
        over & over
those old highways & iron

bridges, those bridges, those
bones of giants spanning crownlike
town to town, etchings of my own
        crossings, uncrossings, small the glimmer
        of me again, leaving again
above the expectant water.

CHILDHOOD BEDROOM, THIRD TOWN

Praise afraid to cut her hair,
& praise the penknife
she uses only for good, for opening

stitches that haven't been made
straight, for cutting
envelopes or shapes

in styrofoam. Praise
the ugly pink sponge-
painted walls, like the inside

of a lung, mottled, geranium-
bright, the made bed, the window
& the power lines

that might have been a tree.
Praise flat on her back.
Praise always. Praise the books

chimneyed & spilling
under her bed, & how the bed catches
that exact magic-carpet

square of sun. Praise the oddness
of being up here mid-
morning. Praise dust *motes*,

a new word, the micro-cities
she pictures on the backs
of those flecks that catch the day-

light & go up
in white flame. Praise destruction
in the streets,

the book about the bomb, mutation
dreams & the ground
it has leached into,

praise pneumonia
& breast buds, praise the suspicion
weapons are hid in her own chest, praise the game

about the crow in the back alley
who sits on the lines & calls
hoarse & constant

toward the house, & how
she started talking
back that year, & how

it came about one night he
was at that window & said
          No time to explain

& she understood.
Praise how she rode
his slippery night-blue body

over the coal stacks, cracked
windows, West Allis—land of small
yards, of libraries, of stained

limestone, land of surveillance, of short-of-
breath, land of can't-get-far.
Praise how he brought her back.

NOTHING LISTENS OVERHEAD

I grew breasts in my garden,
I found bones beneath
my tongue—leftovers
from the river demon my father caught
when the Mississippi
flooded, freshwater
trenches of meat
we picked with wet fingers.
Pin bones,
sharp as hair. He cut off

the human-looking parts.
The hunting guns hummed
in a locked closet. In the sky,
pictures of missing women
hung, unspeaking. And I
grew breasts, ate
the Johnny jump-ups,
muddy at the knee,
I chewed their trusting
blue faces. I cut open pearl

onions, thinking of eyes.
I was the elder
daughter, eavesdropping
at the top of the stairs, coin-
counting, combing the mist
from my sister's hair.
I studied murder
ballads for their plot.
There were princesses, once,
chained to the rocks, the better to feed

whatever swallowing spirit
would emerge to pick them
clean, leave only
stars on a clear night behind.
I sang a hymn,
my mouth a carving knife,
about how it would not be me.
The guns could hear me,
at the back of the closet.
The soup rose to a boil.

GIFT OF TONGUES

Snaked from drain-pipe throat gutter god-grunt or
grammar Latin, Dad glossolalias
          angel language, act
               of spasm, muscle-
                      mouthed brogue, Big Bang waves
—& I see a dark body lean over
him, it seems, & am afraid. Is it right
          to put the Lord to
               name, to so-&-so
& crescendo and if so could I? I

try. I say the stammers, slack-lipped, garbly.
          Dad says I blaspheme.
But he will pray I get it. I am 6
          years old. Dinnertime,
               say thank-you-Jee-sus-
for-this-food-&-thankyouforeverything-
          amen. Time gutters,
goes to a street in Boston where Dad plays
schizophrenic, sputters curses to clear
the crowd before us. I am afraid, god,

          of dying like he
               did, gone beyond gone,
bygone shotgun gumcrack ash-in-a-bag,
& the loom & sneer I saw standing once
over him praying, & my own birdsong
          drowned-out warning—here,
               spring again, I am
                    sweet, claustrophobic
(didn't I dream then of gold rungs, angels
          going up, air all

          of an open) in
the service where some off-key priest repeats
          holy holy hol—

POEM WITH EYES & A KNIFE

Here is the bus stop
where dad drops us off,
where we will wait the 8 promised

minutes for the last bus back
to our hotel across town.
He lives here because the rent's cheap
& he likes the locals, he says, how at home
they are. At the corner bar,

he bought us cokes, & a round for the room,
sampling their slang. He ordered rum & pineapple juice
when they'd turned away.

Earlier, he gave us money to get ourselves
dinner—too much
of it—handing me hundreds
behind the wall of the sculpture garden.
Don't draw attention. I feel like a John.

Maybe my little sister
wouldn't know what that means.
I am the elder daughter.

Here at the bus stop,
Bobby isn't looking to go
anywhere. He's lived in this neighborhood
all his life, homeless now, but still
here & good

to talk to, my dad says, introducing us.
Old, with knuckles
grandmother-like, as if he's held

a wood spoon for much of his life,
he tells us we have Irish eyes.
Dad tells him to watch out
for us, then leaves
for the night.

Next morning, packed to go home, we'll wait
in Dad's truck while he cries, the only time
I've seen it happen, fat sloppy drops wetting his face

—a rock in the desert, struck open—
I'm becoming such a sap.
Six months later, he'll rig a shotgun
so he can pull the trigger
while the barrel's in his mouth.

They'll mail us his boxes:
cigarette butts, blank paper. I'll find
a powdered mirror, his dented pocketknife,

half a paperback
of *The Dharma Bums*, only one
brown bloodstain,
but I'll say there were more,
telling this story.

I'm a sentimental old man,
he said in his truck that day, & we two daughters
were afraid to comfort him.

Here is the stop where we wait.
It is close to midnight.
Here is the street, candescent
with old rain, fresh-stubbed
cigarettes, stars out

overhead, those sterling pneumatic tubes
shipping light from the long past
to us, waiting, & because

I am the eldest, I turn to Bobby.
You don't have to stay.
We can take care of ourselves.
& Bobby, who is holding, now,
one grandmother hand against the other, says,

I know you can, girls & leaves.
But we see him, stalling, watching out,
at the corner of the street.

FOURTH TOWN

       June & we carry
the pack of one
lucky cigarette
down Main Street, bridge

spiders trembling in new webs,
beyond the end
of houselights, into
grass, asphalt, brush

that greets us with its teeth,
the after-rain bloom, dog-mouth
night & the river.
Frogspawn. Spume. Speaking

tongues, licking our feet.
And the moon's had its only eyelid
sliced off, can't help itself
but stare.

       This is the last town, the one
I can't leave.
My sister lights the cigarette.
Passes its rabbit-eye flame

to me & I drag
the good smother
down. (At home
the tv preacher yawps on

about doomsday.)
       I'm there—my sister
on the banks, & me,
trying to get some message to

the river, water that rises
& seeps up
into our house on Main Street
when the rains come—

      Go back, go back, go back,
I'm trying to tell it. (At home the sympathy
lilies wilt like paper burning.)
Go back, go back,

go back we're still not ready.

▽

DROWNING

Begin at the beginning: corkbodied, me:
surf-stolen. There are many ways to lose

a little girl. One: teach her to say *Our Father*
on cue. Two: call her sharp-tongued & willful.

Three: let her swim out too far alone, until
she turns into a cupped ear the sea pours through.

Grandmother Bitchsong, yawn at amen, this water may
curse & spit as it please. It has cut its teeth on empires;

it already knows me. Four: snatch her out
on time. Soothsayer, old-boned Pacific, a pounce-span

from taking me, was thwarted by my own mother, bomb-
builder-raised Navy brat, begging her daughter back. Five:

shout a spell against rip tide, against a home I didn't know
was mine until it wouldn't let me go.

WEEPING FIG

Adam found the first black widow
pacing a dry shadow, near the redwood plank
we walked to its trunk, over furniture limbs, particle
board—all that aged, leaf-freckled, heaped debris.
We'd found ways to stay above it

or to the edges, where we made
a counter & a stovetop, & kept
a few dented pie tins, & a pot
that turned water rusty & coin-flavored.
There was wood enough, & light

—not shade like other trees—redder,
like eyelid light, like something used.
We balanced the long beam to the center.
Climbing, we picked out our bedrooms. And I had
the high flat branch with a window to the yard. I was lookout.

Lunchtime, when my dad found out Brit's splinters
weren't bleeding like they should, he swore he'd drink
peroxide if she let him pour it on her palms.
She opened her hands out over the grass.
Sound of whimper; sound of foam.

Then back to the underneath, big as god, a house
of drooping leaves, where we had a swing—half-finished,
a hard yellow rope fastened to an upper branch,
loop knotted at the end. We'd put one foot in, hold high,
stand back, push off, fly.

And when Olivia stepped on a nail
we were sure had pierced some ancestor's foot
—it looked red as a relic, even before
her blood began to print the dirt—we didn't tell that time,
but tied a piece of towel where it hurt.

And when our speechless grandmother lurched in
to sigh & moan about the dangers there, we scattered
like a snake discovered, & I would run
the farthest, though the fruit trees, magnolia, scrub pine, to the edge
of the desert, breathing & racing & turning

back, I'd go back
under the tree where I was alone. Alone
I stepped in & swung, my quickness
cut the light, while somewhere she wailed for me—
                                    but that can't be right.

It must've been the funeral visit
when Dad washed Brit's hands.
And it happened after, often,
I was alone & swinging, & true
it wasn't safe. More than once, by mistake

or wonder at what
would come, I let go
& let that tree
drag, & scrape, & dangle me
ankle-first along the ragged world…

            I think there is a monster named Remember
& its mouth is a looped rope.
How else am I still hanging, hair turned root,
& she hasn't come
clawing & keening to find me?

THE GREAT WAVE

Suspension: the boats in its singing crib. Sea, a silk rope
slipping through a fist. Mother's milk. Nervous swallow
tucked in each human throat. How the fishing boats

swallow, still
buoyant, sensing slip—hair, snarl, a space
the earth ties to itself. Suspension: the boats, each one

a planet in the open water.
How it can be calm as a green enameled dinner plate
one instant, the next strikes.

How a boy holding a lightning bug
in the cup of his palm
is gentle, so as not to jolt it into opening

its wings. Its boat-body,
polished ebony & trusting.
How his fingers rise

careful, then come down swift
to squish it. Something sings in the underground.
Plates shift.

And how I tried it too. How I reveled in the smear
of moonguts across my palm. How I wanted that light
to be my light, suspended

in the empty sky, which, like sea, is fathomless
& darker as you go—
a stack of plates smashing apart. Hands

slip. We don't mean this small
violence. It must have been
a hundred generations of men who hit their sons

in my family. How do you undo
that smear, put the glow back in its source? And anyway, I am
no son, but vessel, boat

& ocean: a salt-beast, brine-thirsty, & the buoyant
container. I want no part of it.
But I closed my palm too.

Suspension: how it must have sounded, rising
backward & upward, the span, the slipknot
closing. Not like a smash, but singing.

THE WHITHER-THOU-GOEST CURSE

Don't let him come back,
I said when the cops came.
We were unreeling

toward the Pacific that summer
& I was so mad, stuck in a desert

motel room & my mother's bruises
hardly showed at all.
They'd never keep him.

But I took his ring—fat-banded & heavy
in my pocket, her promise
inscribed inside: *Whither thou goest*

I will go. A spell against the pull
of instinct, toward

flatlands, older cities, backward—my mother
in her straw hat, swatting flies &
weeding the garden

—into
landlock & snow
she followed. Don't

let him come back—by miracle
I could read maps, get us west

& then wester—the Painted Desert,
Petrified Forest, that spot on the highway
we stopped for my brother to puke

into the Mojave & nothing
for miles but signs
warning of rattlesnakes—

through Barstow with its wig stores
& waterless yards, up into

the seed-bead night—stars
in the mountains.
It's possible

       sometimes to do it right,
to break it. Look,
I'm just 16 & I know

I've got the ugly go-now instinct
in me too. The whole big country

& its roads, motels,
its deserts of shell
fossils & stars—all of that

       is on my tongue.
The right words,
the prophecy:

It won't get any better.
Don't let him come back.

It was mine then: the spell
of time on that road west,
the between of it, that homeland.

Take it please: flames
        in each tree, monarchs roost
        in the palms one morning
on their way elsewhere, wings
        like light on closed eyes,
shush of their million red shadows.

Lift your tongue & let me
        put memories, warm
        sentence-boned riverbed settle
to the lisp & pith of me: that dream
        there lived a witch at the end
of the courtyard, & the suddenly

enough words I had to tell it.
        And so I remembered.
        And so she was mine.
And so I was a coathanger, a word
        I couldn't say but wore
the unbuttoned pink corduroy out

where they'd flown already, thin
        candlelight cloud—I missed it.
        If you would please just
take these lesser heartbreaks, the slip
        of hair twist & how to wrap loose
pieces to pretend they're food, put in your mouth my

misunderstandings: *how do you make*
        drumsticks mommy take a bone wrap some meat
        around it & put it in the pot? Here, have
the Tale of Mrs. Tiggywinkle, her
        hob & brogue—if I could just
take off my skin pool-damp & give it to her

to wash like soiled clothes!—but I, I overgrow
        the yellow swimsuit, pull hair from my temple
        when I've run out of loose.
Take it please, just do: small
        hedgehog-hole self & what hangs
outside: lines of clean linen

WALKING THE LAND

My grandmother uncoils
her long hose across

the yard, & at her side I go
with her to water the trees

each sundown. Shrub yews
& ornamental juniper,

bitter & mineral, with a bowl
worn at each of their feet,

whittled by hosewater, by being attended to
each evening. Her ancestors,

on Halloween nights, did something
like this: walking

the land, reading its signs,
watching for a message in the flock

of snow geese as they crossed
the horizon. My grandmother

picks up a fallen orange
& pockets it for breakfast.

She tugs at the hose
like a horse's neck-rope——come along.

A young woman, she moved
west, wore her mouth

victory red, sat at the end
of the factory line,

counting the new bombs. They shone
like the blaze of ball lightning

at the peak of the new barn
each summer of her childhood, rumored

in town to be her mother's ghost.
And I have to imagine

she, the seventh daughter
of a seventh daughter, spoke

to the apparition, secretly,
imagine she almost knew

by instinct how to swallow
its light & beam

outward a path into the future, certain
as motherlessness, & solid

enough to walk on, crackling white-hot
like her family farmhouse, burning

down a little while later—but she ran
from it, west into the hum & shine

of a bomb factory,
tricked herself into not looking at

that burning way, the future
—babies, bricking the front stoop,

coaxing fruit from California
scrub, these watering evenings

& near but not yet, her strokes
like a camera flash, erasing words

for the farm & the ghost & the diaries
that burned.

I want to spit it up:
the whole road I know must be

in the waters of us, spectral
& shining, before & beyond

this evening we face the lemon tree
like a friend we've met at church on All Soul's

Sunday, when she shows me how
to ask nicely if I may take

the good fruit, the ones that shine
like new bombs in its bows,

& we pause in that pooling
minute, as I wonder is it enough

to ask before taking,
though I've never heard the tree cry out

yes, yes, please do—? What sign
are we waiting for—what word

or glint or silence would be
an answer, a proof we are

here, too? As her acre of reclaimed
desert sinks into starlight,

as water glugs into
the cauldron at the root.

DROWNING

But it wasn't my mother
who pulled me out. No,
        it was someone else,
        bony & little as me,
who lifted me

out & back in & out &
into that antique
        glass beneath-world
        again. I didn't know
what it meant until after.

I liked that
tonguey cold suffocation
        while I had her
        coppertasting
mouth working my mouth.

Cold greentinted seawater filled up
my little cokebottle body
        —thrum
        of my heart, Houdini-ing
blood into me—

arrhythmic, a mechanism
designed to fight,
        to buck my way up,
        & break the surface gagging,
to cough up a caul of sea.

Dear mirror, dear drowned
ancestress who kissed too
        hard, lodged the 2 of Swords
        in my lungs, dear
death-by-water, what

sailors get tattoos
to protect themselves against:
       I see you,
       I see you,
wait for me.

DIAMONDS & TOADS

When the lip broke I fell asleep.
Anyway it wasn't my lip. Anyway
I was crossing a bridge over undrinkable water.

When the bruising started I was singing stars
out of hiding. I was coaxing stars
into the shotgun seat. I was driving

& driving. I was forgetting my lines.
I was upping toad & snake with each word
of this story I'd promised to keep mum.

Behind me, over the castle, stole
a century of sleep, deep as a sinkhole
in the desert. The thorns grew unchecked.

What would come out of that mouth
on waking—amphibian, rampant, besmirched?
The thorns grew unchecked.

Once there was a house in the woods that was always in danger of falling down. The mother paid to have it fixed with new beams, but in hurricane season it shuddered all the same. In the basement, the water rose up.

The father was a gold ring in a cup. The children slept through daylight in odd corners, sometimes a cat lain like a holy book beneath one palm.

The eldest daughter had a car old enough to drink legally, & she loved it like a talking horse. She watched the dials, popped the hood, unscrewed the reservoir & filled it to the lip with burning blue antifreeze straight from the jug. She loved how she could take care of it like that—could open its surface & look at the parts: which were hurt, & which were doing fine. This is a story about fixing things on time.

Once the mother said, *if you leave again, don't bother coming back*. The eldest was always about to leave, so she took the Atlas of North America, her dad's Swiss Army knife, the wool blanket, & the copy of *1001 Arabian Nights*. When she was in danger, the atlas wouldn't sing. The blanket threads did not quicken time. What she took was out of spite.

At night, she idled by the back gardens of big houses, shut her headlamps, took down their hose, watered her car & snuck away. During the day, curled in sun & pollen on the front seat, parked by the river, she found ways to sleep.

She dreamed of broken floors, loose teeth, a horse skull that speaks & speaks.

WRECKS

This is the kind of moon
men are killed under.
Matchflame in the sky, waxing

gibbous, wildernessing
the land below. Upstairs,
my brother is saying
he wants to die.
On the highway to the west
of us, there is a wreck.

A cicada goes off
like a gas leak somewhere.
In the downstairs bathroom,
naked, I am cutting my hair.

TATTOOS CAN BE USEFUL

For instance your body can be a recipe for becoming more your body.
How you tell yourself the story before it happens:

this one will mean I passed through thorny places safely; here the sea spills from me.
How folks ask which hurt most. How you look like you might win a fight.

For instance a tattoo over your heart feels exactly like heartbreak, the same
dull burn on the sternum & when it heals the old beat flutters up

like the insect you had engraved there
so the world would know what it was dealing with—a lightbulb-loving

sweep against a cheek, anxious for fire. Because certain spells only work
if you carry them in the open, like ABRACADABRA cures bubonic plague

& some spells need two skins, yours & your sister's, & you told the artist
you were twins when she was sixteen with a doctored birth certificate but it
    worked—

the spell worked, the way they do, in jolts & shudders & how you drove
two hours to see her in the ward, how there

she was in low old sweatpants & a wifebeater with birds on it, how there
they were, the dark words on her hip, matching your wrist,

& she was crying, she was saying
get me out of here, but you left when you were told, drove

all night, pulsing across state lines, & your car broke down
finally at 4 a.m. & mom had told you don't come home.

How teeth on teeth you were on your friend's floor, talking in your sleep
    —I'm sorry I'm sorry—   Once you wanted to make your skin

do magic: bird on one side, cage on the other, it works
on a forearm in the right light, I swear it does, you move fast enough

the bird jumps in, but that summer
you were so fucking sick of jumping from cage to cage

you walked one day all fifteen miles to the next town to get it covered
with something bigger, more corvid, & flying away.

TO AN '89 SOFT-TOP CHEVY CAVALIER

Duct-taped,
        undying,
                the most all-mine

thing I ever had, with your
        janky ignition, your leaks,
                the mildew & riverweed

abloom in your backseat
        where I lay under a thin quilt
                with the top down in November

& watched meteors skim
        the night like a struck match.
                Rag & exoskeleton

chariot with a cracked rearview,
        we knew the wayplaces,
                the gloaming bloodsuckers,

brown bats, fog drift, fox-eye, rushlight
        caught in the highbeam, the road through
                the Gorge, past the hundred-year-old

trainwreck, or that sketchy bend
        by the abandoned boyscout camp,
                where in spring a man had sat down

with a gun & a beer
        & all day while the cops closed off the town
                looking for a missing

person or a body, you & I
        stuck to the unpatrolled
                shortcuts & dangerous bridges

waiting for him to make up his mind
so we could go home.
Summer after

the rainstorm, I lit two cigarettes, passed one
to the boy under the hood,
got him stoned good

for making you spark & fire,
for putting in the new valves.
I gave you hose water

when there was no antifreeze.
I tried to hotwire you
when I lost my keys.

And when the nights began
lengthening, I drove
to every North Jersey

town that had a shop for witches
& bought lovage leaves,
benzoin, rue.

I left day-old loaves
at crossroads on the new moon,
praying hard

for an out, an ending,
for uncross me
uncross me uncross me—

while in the harvest mud parked
dog-faithful
like always you kept guard.

STRAY

My mother says I'm like a cat
she feeds but it comes back

less often. Each night my bed
changes. She thinks some blood

curse or moon cycle thing
compels me to keep wandering

off again, but I don't think it's that.
I think the world is flat

as a mattress. I think I miss

its outer edges even when I can't
get far. I think I want

to sleep like that old song
in the pines tonight alone,

the redhead yawning shadow
a patrolman thought he saw; tomorrow

with a young man one town over
whose chest is always warm. And winter

will come on, all bleached sheet breakfast snowfalls.
Sorry mom. I know I oughta call.

HEARTSEASE

Love, the blue-brown juice that pools beneath

the smack to the ribs. Love, the file of vitals,

the bloodspot like a bad pressed flower.

Love the memory-charm, mornings

of early frost & burning red diesel—blue, brown

—a broken pipe, a bruise, a bit of ice—

love. Don't make me again, it says. My feet

against the radiator, which worked that winter.

Love, the juice over the eyes, the cupboard-vinegar

I dashed into a pot to tang the stew. Love, the bluing, the trick

to cover evidence of stains in sheets. Love,

the bluing. Don't make me again. Love, the arrow

that misses the heart, spills endless blue-brown

diesel gallons on the ground,

& love, the thousand, thousand years that it will take

to halve such a mistake, cover the stain; love,

the sweet liqueur that made me hesitate

to steal the matches, cinder that place; love,

the reasoning to not escape,

& when I did, love, that path to her door,

past the greenhouse where birds flew

into glass that looked like air, then lay

wide-eyed in the impatiens, as if just waking up

to a monstrous face they were compelled to yearn for.

SPRING COMES IN THE FORM
OF FEVER DREAMS

Driveway awash, my car's bottom
ruts the rocks. *I counted thirty vultures in the spruce,*
my mother says & rubs the crack in her
thumb knuckle. Soapy hyacinth bloom
& white ammonia on the countertops.
I'm not saying I believe in omens but.

Bathtub a lifeboat I fill to the rim,
add salt & rosemary. Cough like taking out the bobby pin
that holds it all up. Taffeta-black carrion fowl
perch on the roof, while on the porch
I drink weak coffee, while water runs from the eaves.
I'm like a cat she feeds but it comes back less often.

With my mud-damp floormats & exhaust leak, yes, that's me,
the one who always leaves. The radio broadcasts a flood watch
then Thunder Road. *I'm here to pick you up.*
We climb chainlink & let go, tumble to the dead
weeds around the municipal watertower, dry now.
Go up slow, foot slips, cold drip from above.

On the eye of it we smoke in the stormlight.
Below us, bald-budded trees
& what melts. The floor slopes edgeward to a long fall.
If you die at the end of winter
does your winter never end?
            Height-sick, I give him my keys

& roadhead on the shortcut.
At the A&P, chicken for soup.
At his parents' a cup of Throat Coat
& movie about shipwreck.
I've been picturing the afterlife all wrong
—a flooded campsite, climb over chainlink

to a fireweed meadow, the farm's garbage furrow
my grandmother in her girlhood found, corpsehair filled
hairbrush, blonde prairie wind, orphanhood that gets in the blood.

Hot to the touch, he says. Nervous
gas flame in the kitchen to brew a second cup
                    —St. Elmo's Fire
that hissed on her homestead—   there's thunder
at the door. *I can't tell if you're watching or asleep.*
Out the window, rain eats the world.

PRAYER

Put in me the pathways,
            the neural zings
to make me believe in you. Put me into spring
storms with no umbrella. Make it rain for days

until the rails wash out, then leave me in the train
            station in Newark. Let no one pick up their phones
& crowd the place with yuppies commuting to flood zones,
the supine man with waterlogged blue eyes, the same

woman who told me she was pregnant
            3 years ago—*just down on my luck.*
God bless you, honey—I gave her my last 10 bucks
once, but she doesn't know me now. *Please, for the baby, even 50 cents.*

Put in me the stupid sparrow heartbeat that wants
            to get back to a home
I wish I could get out of. Put in me good strong bones,
clear eyesight, a gut that can take hunger & the will to not

be stranded—bless me with legs, a thumb,
            a sketchy ride.
Drunk drive me through the water: roads alongside
drowning ditches, new houses in their sleep, rivers overrun.

Put a knife in my pocket;
            make me get back safe
to somewhere I'm unwelcome. Put in me my life—
each deadly clear-skied after-morning of it,

fresh as a cold sweat.
            Hold me under. Give me all I get.

PRACTICAL ADVICE FOR WAYWARD DAUGHTERS FACING FAIRYTALE MONSTERS

1. There are rules. There are always rules. There is always a walled garden to climb out of, or a churchyard you must walk widdershins. There is always a rune-blessed doorway to cross through. There is always a path that twists into darkness beneath the castle, & the wild beast at its center, always waiting to feast on you.

2. You were not meant to survive it. You must be clever, & carry a ball of string, or breadcrumbs to lead you out again. You must be brave, & willing to escape a different way than how you came. It will change you, this journey. It will make you strong; it will make you jump at loud noises & forget how to unlatch the muscles of your back.

3. There are rules; there are always rules. There is always the freak spring snow, thick around your ankles, as you stand on the bridge out of town, placing a call to the girl you're in love with. Sometimes she's told you she loves you, too, in a voice you called *lilting* when you first heard it over the phone. There is the path that twists into darkness. There is the bridge & your sodden ankles. There is your mouth, saying, *My dad just killed himself*, & her mouth somewhere else, saying, *But why are you calling me?*

4. If you have never had someone to hold you through disaster before, you better find them quick. You better wait up all night as she loses her way driving to your town. You better be ready with directions. It is the string you hold in the dark, these someone-else's arms around you. Before this, you might have been telling yourself stories about how you can survive anything. No one gets through a night like this alone.

5.   You were not meant to survive it. The monster will scent you out. The monster is a bullet in the brain. The monster is in the boxes, delivered to your front porch on the first day of thaw. A bird is building a nest in the eaves. It goes back & forth, carrying twigs from the dogwood tree. You go back & forth, carrying inside the boxes of his papers, his books, his personal effects. There is the pocketknife you remember him using to cut picnic sandwiches in half. Back & forth. The first nice day. The bird is keeping an eye on you. It hasn't decided you are safe.

6.   It will scent you out. Sometimes it will possess her, & she will call you from her dorm room, talking about wanting to die. You are so distant from her now, she says. You are so cold. It will scent you out. *I'm so cold, I'm so cold*, you tell her on the phone. *I'm so scared.* You are dreaming every night of taking out your organs & putting them in baskets made of seagrass. You are lighting every candle you own; you are leaving scorch marks on the windowsill. You are sending up flares that say, *Save me.* That say, *You said you loved me.* That say, *Please don't let it come back.*

7.   There is always a center, & your own feet to take you there. There is always a day she will make plans to swallow a bottle of pills, & you will spend all your money getting on a train to see her. There is always the journey between, the train a silk string. She leans like a cowboy on the wall of the station, waiting to pick you up, & you wonder if she was lying about wanting to die. You wonder if she was trying to get back at you for how you had no one else to call that night on the bridge. Driving you back to her campus, she'll get worried you don't exist. *What if I'm crazy?* she'll ask.

What if I'm talking to no one. What if you're all in my head.
She'll refuse to look at you, or speak, for hours & hours.

8.   You will go hungry. The maze is long. You are out of money, & she isn't bringing you cafeteria food as she promised. You wander her campus all day while she is in class. Once you come upon a conservatory & dozens of finches, dead in the garden. They have broken their necks against the walls of clean glass. Know then you are near the center.

9.   It will find you in her muggy basement dorm room, as you sit facing her on the twin bed, & you see mirrored in her eyes a hunched, patient shadow over your shoulder, & you see she sees it; you see she is so afraid of what sits behind you there & you are afraid, too. And then you are not.

10.   When you face the monster, you must say hello in a language it knows.

11.   You must not get close until it lets you, & then you must have a knife in your back pocket, just in case.

12.   You must give it the knife. It belonged to him anyway. You must place yourself within arm's reach & not flinch.

13.   This is the only protection spell worth a damn. To not flinch when it looks you in the eye.

STRING

I bind to me the knack of the survivors:
the edge ecologies: mugwort, blackberry,

radon-eating fungi, fireweed, & flies
making up a hum-chant near the alley cans.

I bind my own bad mouth & bitch instinct

to talk back to the future, bind the fetch
of my grandmother, standing at the foot

of my bed one October night, refracted,
every age at once, saying goodbye.

I tie her face into my own. I'm sure

there is a way to hold this present—a string
of words, spun gold & certain as a knot,

to tighten on the disappeared, secure.
And why should I not be the one to find it?

TIME MAGIC

In the beginning, time works like a snake

born from the throat of a maid: spell of dry season, of hot-between-
the-thighs, spell of forked tongue & womb
where red embers wrap together, like hair around a finger.

TIME MAGIC

An accident: lightning & amino acids,

dog-bark-tide-twist under a sky

of antique glass. Saltwatered, a fresh cell

opens its mouth. But nobody likes a tattle-tale.

TIME MAGIC

Bedraggled, bearing a torch broken off

the lightning-struck spruce, she mixes the warm stormwaters of her mouth
with red clay, to paint her dream of aurochs. The spell works like that: it
   holds

the world together by spit & clay & stolen fire.

TIME MAGIC

The spell works like that: it twins the tongue, twines sea to sternum
crack. Undo its wrap, & it will always coil back

like well-spun flax. Let every spit-born daughter
try to tell it, turn it out of air. It will always rewind to the once upon.

Uncauldron me. Uncaulk the ship
my father sailed at summer camp. Uncurl
my mother's hair. Somewhere primordial, the thaw
begins. There's blood on the yolk of the moon.

TIME MAGIC

Cassiopeia hangs in the midheaven, the Papesse sleeps

at the top of the deck, & my mother, in the kitchen,
ties back her hair to punch down

the bread. *If you leave again, don't bother coming back.*

TIME MAGIC

Tell about the sea: a heart, green & made for leaping.

Tell about the habits of lightning: how the whole house

would shake, trying to get the sound off its back.

About the stars: a road of ash we get to follow.

TIME MAGIC

Unweave the linens. Undiscover fire, return
the lightning to the air. Be careful what you wish for,
coos Hesperus in the serrated west. We'll go back,

west, someday, too. I can't help myself. I choose it all again.

VIA COMBUSTA

"If the moon is in the burned place…then it will not be good if you decide anything according to this." — DOROTHEUS OF SIDON

This is the season girls go missing, sleeping in beds not their own.

One bolts awake, speaking a dead language. One is drinking bad wine from the bottle in a floodwater parking lot. She raises her collar like wolf hackles against the cold.

The band paid one to lie in a beautiful coffin all Halloween night as they played their show, red-nailed hands crossed neat over the heart. She is bleeding on schedule, & she is silent. Her black lace dress won't show a stain.

One is the moon, who travels the sorcery road this time of year. One is a heart, & one is a red nail. One is the key to her mother's old house. She will bleed when she's set in a lock without permission. She is on schedule, silent.

One is taking a shortcut between towns when the radio cuts out—then in the after-hiss, her own voice wobbles through, asking a question she can't pick up. The freaked flare of a fox splits the road—she swerves too fast & catches a skid—the high school's lit sign whips by (*TIME MANAGEMENT CLASSES*).

This is the way—snow bends into star—the road unfolds, opens, becomes, suddenly, full of girls. Their eyes, multiplicitous in the dark windshield, are flames/ keys/ hers, suspended mid-swerve.

Then just as quick, the wheel is back in her control; the road beneath her; animal safe on the other side. The static cuts in, spangled & talismanic: her own heart, thrumming.

The voice is gone. She waits to hear it again.

SHARING A BED

Some nights I have slept with the long, matted braid
of a different woman down my back, borrowed dress
wrinkled at her hips, or else with a cat

whorled by my ear, or dog solemn at my feet.

There have been nights I forgot it gets so cold
this late in spring, when my bed was a tilted shotgun
seat, or grass gully by freight rails, & I shared it with missed

calls from my mother asking where I am.

Once I wanted to marry her: colt-footed
& not quite human after nightmares, I'd climb in.
I am still that thing in her doorway

on a night at the end of summer, as the Santa Anas begin.

But since then, I have slept with
escape plans, go-bag on the nightstand, the sea
flooding my dreams—brutal beginning-of-time rocksalt

in the bones & the tidesmack that wakes me

into the oncoming future, that mishap
of match, blight, or molecule raveling
the air from its hangings, breaking against

one night in the middle of my life. Don't be shy,

dear me that is a different woman,
repairing the dark in my wake. I still have a ring
of keys to every home I've ever known, sleeping beside me.

They will bleed if they are put to the right lock.

QE

LAND OF CAN'T-GET-FAR

All runaways come home, eventually.
Each pauses on the stoop to look at stars
          like spilled milk, ejaculate, unraveling bridal

veils, mushroom spores, exponential keyhole lights—
that unfinished business. While somewhere, a caterpillar
          weaves itself a pure silk transformation room;

somewhere, a hungry dog sneaks into church
to steal the god-bread from the altar plate;
          somewhere, a mother is teaching her son

to balance on a rail by using feet as eyes
& keeping his eyes fixed on the middle distance.
          See how the stars don't care the ways we yearn

or don't yearn toward them? Is that love—? To know
nothing is waiting, & still step forward?

LITTLE RED RIDINGHOOD'S
GOT SOME LEGS ON HER

That mouth that mouth that dirty mouth of yours,
says the man who follows me
by the bright of my wool

coat into the station. Praise be
my fuck-offs, praise the electricity
in me, the jolt that understands

how to unsnare, keep walking, double
back out the threshold; praise how this time it's easy
to break his gaze, to bow my head & pass

into the rain's shudder & bloom.

                    •

In my mother's house there are many rooms.

There are hollows, ceiling leaks,
meadowflower & wolf-den-
musk scented sheets. I am small

& cold as a penny.
She feeds me tea and cake.
She wants me to try on her wedding dress.

This was my grandmother's china. This is the wine
she bought but can't get open. This is the mean jaw
of spring, a draft under the door. She's taken

to bolting it at night. This is the snare
I can't break free of: here
by witchcraft, cream silk, crawl

space, tooth & nail, this is the land
where I remint myself,
reduce; I'll tell her nothing

but good news: my smart haircut,
the new coat bought on sale.
Am I happy am I

hungry am I keeping warm. Mom I'm keeping
one step ahead for now. I bow
my head, accept the glass she pours.

FORECLOSURE

Sometimes the ghost appeasement spell
works like this: your mother locks the door
for the last time. She's glad, she says,
the bank took the house. It was too
big to clean with her bad ankles.

The radio kept coming on at midnight.
The candles went out of their own accord.

And that river! By stovepipe or basement wall,
it got in—long-legged, stealthy, breathing
at keyholes, loping & fingering the knob
of the closet where the guns were kept.
At the foot of the stairs, it wept.

Gather 10 years of a bad mortgage,
ash & bone chips in a plain brown box, & the last day
you'll cross the bridge together, drown them in the fishing spot.

You leave a beeswax votive
lit on the flat rock, & wade back through
the water—that river!—headrush, gibberish, home-no-more, memory
of the night you woke in the ectoplasm
of some hurricane, & followed the moonlight down

to the front door thrown open, glass & dogwood petals
strewn across the rug, like someone has just returned
from a long trip, desperate to tell the whole story.

LETTER FROM MY YOUNGER SELF

It has been raining for weeks,
& I can hear the foxes in the weeds
being brave by being silent.

At the back of the clouds, the stars
have been in a bad mood for most of my life.

This is a town of mill fire
& iron bridge, & its first mayor lived here
in this house. Sometimes I think it's haunted

by other versions of me. I sit as a fox
at the window, meeting the eye of an empty

room. I have asked the stars tonight to make a road
from them to this place to them to you.
It is there for you to use it, whether you want to

or not. Damn but they're riotous
tonight, & me, brave & silent, the only one

awake to feel it. You can get here,
to this floodland & riverish
heartbreak, where I wear thirdhand velvet

& nobody loves me. The world, here, glitters
like ants on roadkill, dissolving

it into something
dark & granular & designified
as ruined film. It's shocking how often

my sister & I go down to the river
at night & both come back unharmed.

(And maybe less shocking
          sometimes we don't.) It has been
a murder ballad for weeks,

& what I really want to know is how
to get to you & how not to—I want to get through

          this catastrophe without growing into
          taxes & fees
instead of stealing to eat, without setting a ring

on my finger & turning over
the Empress whenever I lay down a three-

          card spread—star-crowned
          with a rose gown in the dead grass, she may be
trying to tell you something, but not me. I never

pull her. Until one day, apparently, I do—as I turn
to you, the face at the other side

          of the mirror I use to trick the cards
          into letting me tell my own
fortune—& I know, finally, enough

transformation & I am brave enough & willing,
then, to step the way you stepped

          into the sidereal coincidence that will make me
          you, there, all in that shining
survival, as long as it lasts.

THE LINEN SPELLS

There is a spell to find the right road, to see
in the dark & to pass by day without being seen.
There are spells for not letting a man's head be
cut off, spells for bringing stone animals to life
& for making them plow. For cultivating
& for murder, for seeing far, for traveling by flight.

O so-&-so, the spells go.

O so-&-so, o sod god,
o villain, o charmer, o card cheat.
O weigher of hearts & changer
of sheets. O good host,
o blood-on-the-teeth, o endless &c.

She who breaks the necks of kittens. He who overwaters the roses.
O stranger. O thief.

There's a spell to trick the judges, a spell to pass safely over water, &,
   failing
all else, the spell of transformation, which can change the beloved dead
to a creature that enters
the underworld unnoticed.

O snake, o feline. O long spine, o one who senses the future through its
   nose-tip.
Let me not lose a word of it. Let me slither on through.

POEM WITH OPEN ROADS

Come with me, as if down a highway at night: the flaring strips of yellow, ghostly in their brightness. The whir of the trees above. The way we cannot tell if, ahead of us, are moths or eyes.

Cross forest & desert & cities rippling with the breath of their sleepers. In one town, my mother sits in the dining room of our old house, refilling her cup. The table is lined with a jarful of every ocean I have ever swum in, & near the end, one tips & spills like a filmstrip; we'll follow.

The final girl runs down a hallway the color of blood. The walls are lined with the mouths of dead wives, whispering. The final girl is in the bathroom, dealing with her own blood, when the fight starts. She watches it through the mirror reflecting the cracked door.

What makes you think you are allowed to leave, the fight says. Blood like a jarful of ocean.

Come with me, through mouths that are not mine, through cups & cracked doors, algaea & radiation. Come out the other side, so that when the fires arrive, they will feel familiar—like running down a hallway, rose-bright. Listen, I don't have the words to stop the future, its flood & blaze, but I have (I think) something small & family I can give you: a story of how to open the road.

The final girl is in there, shaking time in her teeth. The ocean is there, & a house beneath it, full of faces & knives. There is a mirror overhead, raining the house down into itself in the form of a thousand glass doll eyes.

It has to count for something I am here, says every drop inside.

ONCE

upon beginning banging on beginning,
stars. I wish that I knew how to tell this
right. Once light & dust unlatching from
a center. Once tide. Once loam & edges;

once fishbone & copper, pestle & plow.
Someone made up the word *mother*
& *dog* & *sing* & *no*. Eventually,
whole stories. What a lucky break: if

some kid later needs to know a path
through curse, or daughterhood, or whatever
you want to call it, I can give them that.

It's yours: the staticky punk song, the shortcut over
the blind bridge, the current underneath.
I cannot tell it right, but I can tell this piece.

THE SOUND OF MY TIME ON EARTH, SPED UP

I'll sing you countdown:
        juke, fluorescent drone, hinge
of a gate rasping open.

I'll sing you Lake Michigan's
        pop & flush, melting; Good
Morning America jingle

& the shantung scratch
        of my mother's penciled
To Do list. Sing a flooded street

one spring & its brass
        refraction, as a catfish,
big as a grown man's foot,

swims by. Mirror, prism, molecule
        of water bending & blotting,
betrothal of soot & ozone,

4 heartbeats
        between lightning & thunder
for each mile distance:

sing you this; sing you mirror
        rattling like teeth
against its hanging

when the thunder hits, mirror
        inherited from my mother
who inherited it

from the beech tree
        cut down to make its frame.
I'll sing you the backside:

beech-woman, combing
            her fresh-washed hair
in the mirror inherited

from all the before;
            sing you the 2 weeks
I spent transformed

into a catfish at age 19,
            inhaling through my knife-slice
gills; sing that form in which I held

a forgiveness that could sever
            like lightning,
the sound of my time

unmothered & numbered, pealing from
            me, 19,
thumbing down a gravel

dead end off Rt. 78; 19, Pennsylvania,
            storm-touched land
unplanted & breathless

in the afterfloods.
            Sing mud & beg
& juke & echo—gunshot

resounding off another
            mountain, storm-touched,
4 heartbeats, footfall

as the woman in the beech mirror walks
            up the underworld stairway
once more into

this my flashpaper place
            hot for the going.
Sing of it: flood, shape-shift,

too much rain
            or not enough; sing of
her, of me, broke free,

back home, kneeling
            in the light & mud to write
a To Do list:

            1.   brood on keepsakes drowned or gone missing
            2.   moon & moon & what could grow here
            3.

NOTES

<u>The Great Wave</u>: after *Under the Wave off Kanagawa (Kanagawa oki nami ura)*, also known as *The Great Wave*, by Katsushika Hokusai. ca. 1830-32, Polychrome woodblock print; ink and color on paper. The Metropolitan Museum of Art, New York.

<u>Tattoos Can be Useful</u>: "Tattoos can be useful or beautiful or a combination of the two. That's reason enough. Sailors used to get images of Christ inked on to their backs to make the first mate reluctant to use the whip on them. They'd ask for elaborate designs on their limbs to mark voyages taken and ports visited – a kind of indelible dog tag that, they hoped, would identify a corpse lost at sea and washed ashore. Every mark had a story." –Jenn Ashworth, in "Painted Ladies: Why Women Get Tattoos." *The Guardian*. 13 December 2013.

<u>Heartsease</u>: otherwise known as the Viola Tricolor, Johnny-Jump-Up, or Love-In-Idleness. c.f. *Midsummer Night's Dream* 2.1.519-561.

<u>Via Combusta</u>: a.k.a. the burning way, the burned path, or the fiery road: an archaic astrological term for a time in October when the sky was thought to be full of ash and bad omens.

Epigraph: Dorotheus of Sidon. *Dorothei Sidonii Carmen astrologicum*, edited by David Edwin Pingree, B. G. Teubner, 1976. pp. 278.

c.f. Louis, Anthony. "The Origin of the Via Combusta (Burned Path)?". *Anthony Louis—Astrology and Tarot Blog*, 28 August 2016.

<u>The Linen Spells</u>: after *Mummy bandage of Hepmeneh, born of Tasheritentaqeri, inscribed with text and vignette from the Book of the Dead*. 332–30 BC. Linen and ink. The Metropolitan Museum of Art, New York.

<u>The Sound of My Time on Earth, Sped Up</u>: after *Numbers (2007)* by Jasper Johns. Aluminum casting. *Jasper Johns: 'Something Resembling Truth'* Feb 10-May 13 2018. The Broad Museum, Los Angeles.

ACKNOWLEDGEMENTS

My gratitude to the publications where these poems first appeared, occasionally in a significantly different form.

Autofocus: "Poem with Eyes & a Knife"
CALYX Journal: "Drowning"
The Careless Embrace of the Boneshaker Anthology (great weather for MEDIA): "The Linen Spells"
Crab Creek Review: "Drowning," "Gift of Tongues" and "The Great Wave"
DIALOGIST: "Once"
Fiolet and Wing: An Anthology of Domestic Fabulism (Liminal Books): "In the Before"
Flash Boulevard: "Via Combusta"
Gigantic Sequins: "Practical Advice for Wayward Daughters Facing Fairytale Monsters"
Gulf Coast: "Land of Can't-Get-Far"
Hypertrophic Literary: "Childhood Bedroom, Third Town"
Indiana Review: "Little Red Ridinghood's Got Some Legs on Her"
Iron Horse Literary Review: "Weeping Fig"
Loud Zoo: "Nothing Listens Overhead" (as "13")
Madcap Review: "Tattoos Can Be Useful"
Pilgrimage Magazine: "Reader" and "The Whither-Thou-Goest Curse"
Radar Poetry: "Alchemy Lesson," "Diamonds and Toads," "Foreclosure," "Heartsease," and "This is a Story About a Heist"
Raleigh Review: "Fourth Town"
Red Paint Hill: "Sharing a Bed"
River Heron Review: "String"
Rust + Moth: "Poem with Open Roads"
Slipstream Magazine: "To an '89 Soft-Top Chevy Cavalier"
So to Speak Journal: "Prayer"
Stirring: A Literary Collection: "Spring Comes in the Form of Fever Dreams"
Storyscape Literary Journal: "Cross Plains"
Switched-On Gutenberg: "Wrecks" (as "This is the Kind of Moon")
The Turnip Truck(s): "We Moved Around a Lot" and "Stray"

I would also like to extend gratitude to the following people, who were integral to the creation of this book.

Donna Masini, Tom Sleigh, and Catherine Barnett, who were early voices of encouragement, and the poets who I had the pleasure of writing alongside in the Hunter MFA program from 2013-2015. Particular thanks to Farryl Last, who read and offered critiques on many subsequent drafts of my poems.

The many writers I've had the opportunity to work with as part of the Creative Writing PhD program at USC: Anna Journey and the poets in her manuscript workshop, Carol Muske-Dukes and the poets who contributed critiques in her craft courses and her Broad reading series, David St. John and the writers and composers who inspired the explorations of the "Time Magic" sequence, Mark Irwin and the poets of his craft course for the sharp advice on titles and opening sequences (despite my stubbornness), and Aimee Bender and her fiction writing workshop (where I drafted several of these prose pieces) for their patience and good humor with having a fiction novice in their midst.

Amy Quan Barry, for the immense gift of choosing this collection for publication.

New American Press and its associates, especially David Bowen, Irfan Jeddy, and Angelo Maneage, for the work and support that gave this book its final form.

Cadu, Ravyn, and all who co-created the poetry path at California Witchcamp, where a couple of these pieces were first drafted.

Whiskey Club for the ice breaking, and for listening to my many check-ins about writing habits and insecurities.

The Goats, for living through it with me.

Mom, for the books she read to me, the books I stole from her, the stories of ancestors, and so much else. Jonathan, for sharing his much-more-scientific understanding of stars and particles. Amelia, forever witch-of-honor, for being unfailingly generous with her wit and perspective.

Josh, for feeding me, for a thousand good conversations, for only rarely complaining about my annoying tendency for getting my best ideas at 1AM. And for all the rest of it.

SARA FETHEROLF is a poet, essayist, librettist, and storyteller. She was born in Southern California, raised in Tornado Country, and came of age amidst the back roads and abandoned factories of western New Jersey. They have an MFA degree in poetry from Hunter College, and they are a candidate in the PhD for Literature and Creative Writing at University of Southern California. She lives in Long Beach, by an unkempt stretch of the Pacific Ocean.

www.ingramcontent.com/pod-product-compliance
Lightning Source LLC
Chambersburg PA
CBHW030850090426
42737CB00009B/1175